Babel Books, Inc.

 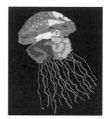 

Children's Illustrated Modern

English-French
French-English

Dictionary

D1501410

By: The Editors of Babel Books, Inc.

Compiled ,Translated by : The Editiors of Babel Books, Inc.

Illustrated by: Yoselem G. Divincenzo

Copyright © 2008 by Babel Books, Inc.

1st Edition

All rights reserved

ISBN 978-0-9800127-5-0

Printed in the United States

For information, address:

Babel Books, Inc.

93-64 204th St.

Hollis, NY 11423

Website: www.babelbooks.us

Introduction

Children's Illustrated Modern English-French/French-English Dictionary was created based on the necessity that every child needs to build self confidence and motivation on the critical years of kindergarten to third grade; as well for adults learning English or French as a second language.

The words utilized were carefully selected to fit into the age-appropriateness. It summarizes how to successfully learn the new language introducing the idea of alphabetical order to be prepared for a higher-level dictionary; containing a variety of everyday words with colorful illustrations that will help children develop interest in letter, sounds, reading and writing. The new colorful art illustrations will bring words to life making the learning process interesting and entertaining.

Introduction

Le Dictionnaire English-French/French-English Moderne Illustré d'Enfants a été créé basé sur la nécessité que chaque enfant doive construire moi la confiance et la motivation sur les années critiques de jardin d'enfants à la troisième qualité; aussi pour les adultes apprenant l'anglais ou le français comme une deuxième langue.

Les mots utilisés ont été soigneusement choisis pour s'inscrire à l'opportunité d'âge. Il résume comment avec succès apprendre la nouvelle langue présentant l'idée d'ordre alphabétique à être préparé à un dictionnaire de niveau supérieur; l'entretien d'une variété de mots quotidiens avec les illustrations colorées qui aideront des enfants à développer l'intérêt pour la lettre, les sons, en lisant et en écrivant. Les nouvelles illustrations colorées d'art apporteront des mots à la vie faisant le processus d'apprentissage intéressant et divertissant.

Contents:

French Pronunciation

		eu	"u" as in English "urge"	on/om	awn as in English "fawn"
a	a as in English "fat"	f	f as in English "farm"	p	as in English "pie"
an/am	an as in English "want"	g	before e or i as s in "pleasure", any other letter as g in "got"	q	k as in English "kite"
b	b as in English in "bed"	gn	y as in English in "Canyon"	r	r as in English "root"
c	s before e or i "facile" k before any other l etter "café"	h	always silent, except "hôtel"	s	s as in English "sad"
		i	ee as in English "feed"	t	t as in in the name "Tom"
c	sh as in English "riche"	j	s as in English "pleasure"	u	u as in English "u" in "cue"
		k	k as in English "kite"		
d	d as in English "doll"	l	l as in English "lamb"	un/um	u as in English "fun"
e	e as in English "sister" (at the end of the word is silent except of the words of one syllabe	ll	y as in English "yes"	v	v as in English "vest"
		m	m as in English "man"	w	w as in English "wet"
		n	n as in English "name"	y	y as an English in "hymn"
é	e as in English "men"	o	as in English "cot"	z	z so the English word pizza is "zebra"
ê	é similar to é	ou	oo as in English "hoot"		

Prononciation Anglaise

				q	co comme dans le français " coing"
a	a comme dans le français "arc"	j	j comme dans le français "jockey"	r	r comme dans le français " rose"
b	b comme dans le français "ballet"	k	k comme dans le français "karate"	s	h comme dans le français "sandale"
c	c comme dans le français "canari"	l	l comme dans le français " lacet"	t	t comme dans le français "train"
d	d comme dans le français "domino"	m	m comme dans le français " masque"	u	ou comme dans le français "douche"
e	e comme dans le français "terre"	n	n comme dans le français " nide"	v	v comme dans le français "violon"
f	f comme dans le français "fleur"	o	o comme dans le français "orange"	w	oo comme dans le français "oiseau"
g	g comme dans le français "gazelle"	p	p comme dans le français " piano"	y	y comme dans le français "yogurt"
h	h comme dans le français " hôtel"			z	t comme dans le français " zebu"
i	i comme dans le français " iris"				

airplane *(air-plihn)*
aéroplane *(ah-eh-roh-plahn)*

alligator *(a-li-ghei-ror)*
alligator *(ah-lee-gah-toh)*

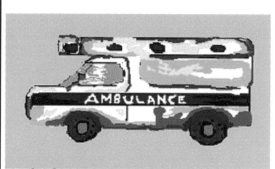

ambulance *(am-bhiu-lahnss)*
ambulance *(ahm-boo-lohns)*

angel *(ewhn-shol)*

ange *(ohnsh)*

ant *(ahnth)*

fourmi *(phor-mee)*

apartment *(a-parth-menth)*

appartement *(ah-pahg-tah-meh)*

apple *(a-pol)*

pomme *(pohm)*

aquarium *(a-coo-eh-rium)*

aquarium *(ah-coo-ah-ree-om)*

5

A

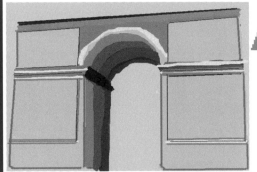

arc *(arc)*   arc *(ahrk)*

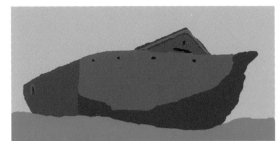

ark *(ark)*   arche *(ahrsh)*

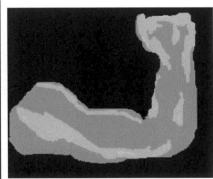

arm *(arm)*

bras *(brah)*

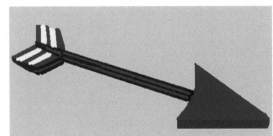

arrow *(e-rrou)*

flèche *(flehsh)*

athlete *(a-tlihth)*

athlète *(ah-tleht)*

automobile *(ah-ro-mo-bil)*
automobile *(oo-too-moh-beel)*

autumn *(o-rom)*

automne *(oo-tohm)*

award *(a-oird)*

prix *(pree)*

B

baby *(bei-bi)*
bébé *(beh-beh)*

backpack
(bhak-pak)

sac à dos
(sahc-eh-doh)

bag
(bag)

sac *(sahk)*

ballet
(ba-leth)

ballet
(bah-leh)

balloon *(ba-loun)*
ballon *(bah-loo)*

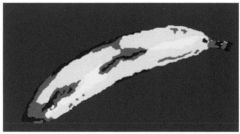

banana
(ba-na-na)

banane
(bah-nahn)

bandage *(bahn-detch)*
bandage *(boh-dahsh)*

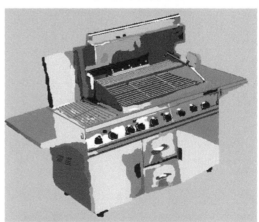

barbecue *(bar-bi-quiu)*
barbecue *(bahr-beh-koo)*

7

B

barn *(barn)*   grange *(grahnsh)*

basket
(bac-keth)

corbeille
(cohr-beh-ee-eh)

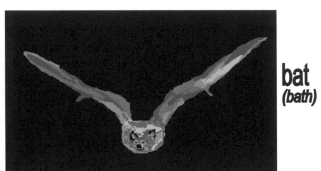

bat
(bath)

chave-souris *(shah-veh/soo-ree)*

battery
(ba-re-ri)

batterie
(bah-tree)

bear *(ber)*   ours *(ohrs)*

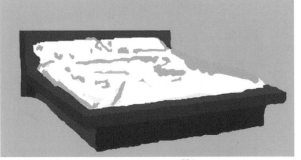

bed *(bedh)*   lit *(lee)*

bee
(bi)

abeille
(ah-beh-ee-lleh)

bell
(bel)

cloche *(clohsh)*

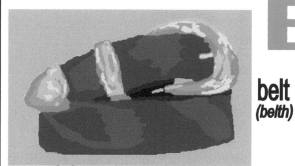

belt *(belth)*

ceinture *(cehn-tee-oor)*

bench *(behnch)*   banc *(bohn)*

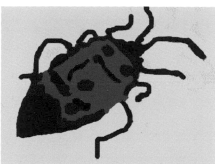

beetle *(bi-rol)*

coléoptère *(coh-lee-ehp-tehrg)*

bicycle *(bahi-si-col)*
bicyclette *(bee-see-cleht)*

binoculars *(bahi-no-quiu-lahrss)*

binoculaires *(bee-noh-kee-oo-lehr)*

bird *(berdh)*

oiseau *(oo-eh-soo)*

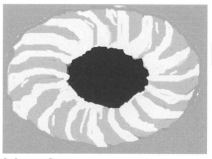

biscuit *(bis-ket)*

biscuit *(bees-kee-oo)*

bison *(bahi-son)*

bison *(bee-zohn)*

9

B

blackberry *(blak-be-rri)*
mûre *(meegr)*

blacksmith *(blak-smeth)*
forgeron *(fohr-sheh-roo)*

boat *(bohuth)*
bateau *(bah-too)*

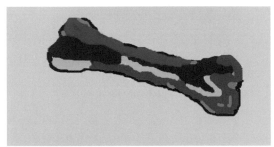

bone *(boh-un)*   **OS** *(ohs)*

book *(book)*

livre *(leevr)*

boot *(boot)*

botte *(boht)*

bottle *(ba-rol)*

bouteille *(boh-oo-teh-ee-eh)*

bouquet *(bou-ke)*

bouquet *(boo-keh)*

bowl *(boh-ool)* terrine *(teh-ree-nah)*

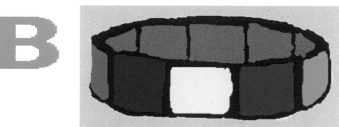

bracelet *(braeh-ihss-leth)*
bracelet *(brahz-leht)*

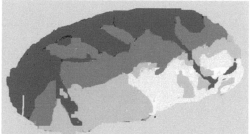

bread *(bredh)*   pain *(pah)*

bricks *(brickç)*

briques *(breek)*

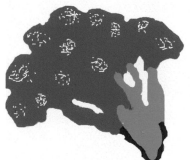

broccoli *(bro-co-li)*

broccoli *(broh-coh-lee)*

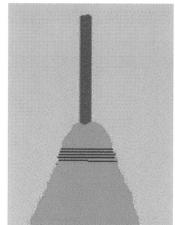

broom *(broum)*

balai *(bah-leh)*

bucket *(ba-keth)*

seau *(soo)*

bulb *(bolb)*

ornement *(ohr-neh-mohn)* 11

B

burglar
(ber-gler)

cambrioleur
(cohm-bree-oh-lehr)

bus *(baç)*   bus *(bee-oos)*

butter
(ba-rer)

beurre *(behgr)*

butterfly
(ba-rer-flahi)

papillon
(pah-pee-yon)

C

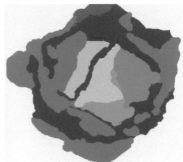

cabbage
(ca-besh)

chou *(shoo)*

cabinet
(ca-bi-neth)

cabinet *(cah-bee-neh)*

cactus
(caktç)

cactus
(cahc-toos)

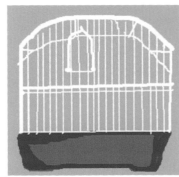

cage
(keish)

cage
(cahgsh)

12

C

cake
(kelik)

gâteau
(gah-too)

calf
(caf)

veau
(voo)

camel *(ke-mol)*   chameau *(shah-moo)*

camera
(ca-me-ra)

appareil de photo
(ah-pah-rehl/deh/phoh-toh)

can
(ken)

boite
(boo-aht)

canary
(ke-ne-ri)

canari
(cah-nah-ree)

candle
(kehn-dol)

chandelle
(shan-dehll)

candy
(kehn-di)

bonbon *(bohn-bohn)*

13

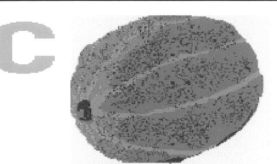

canoe *(ca-noo)*   canoë *(cah-noh-eh)*

cantaloupe *(ken-ta-lop)*
cantaloup *(coh-tah-loo)*

carnation *(car-nei-shion)*
oeillet *(oh-lee-eh)*

carpet
(car-peth)

tapis
(tah-pee)

carrot   *(ke-rroth)*
carotte *(cahg-rroht)*

castle
(ca-sol)

château
(shah-too)

cat
(cath)

chat
(shah)

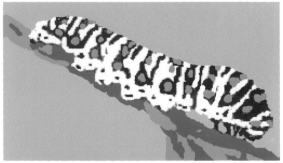

caterpillar *(ca-rer-pi-ler)*
chenille *(sheh-neel)*

14

C

chair
(cher)

chaise
(chehz)

cheese
(chiiç)

fromage
(froh-mahgsh)

cheetah *(chi-ra)* guépard *(geh-pahgr)*

cherry
(che-ri)

cerise
(cehg-rees)

chess *(ché-s)* échecs *(eh-shehk)*

chicken *(chi-kehn)* poulet *(poo-leh)*

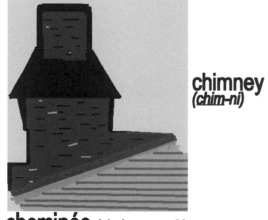

chimney
(chim-ni)

cheminée *(sheh-mee-neh)*

chimpanzee
(cim-pan-si)

chimpanzé *(sheem-pahn-zee)*

15

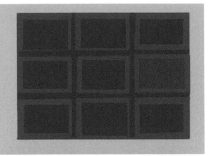

chocolate *(cho-co-leh-ith)*
chocolat *(shoh-coh-lah)*

C

church *(cherch)*

église *(eh-gleez)*

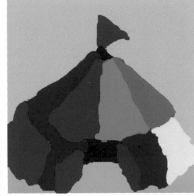

circus *(cir-cu-s)*

cirque *(seerk)*

clock *(clock)*

horloge *(ohr-lohsh)*

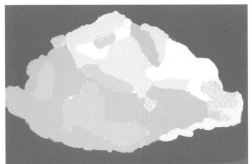

cloud *(clah-oud)*   **nuage** *(nahsh)*

clown *(clah-oun)*

clown *(cloon)*

cobweb *(cob-web)*

toile d'araignée *(too-ehl/dahg-rahg-nee-eh)*

coconut *(co-co-noth)*

noix de coco *(noo-eh/deh/coh-coh)*

comb
(kohmb)

peigne
(pehg-nee-eh)

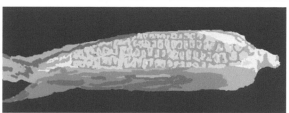

corn *(corn)*　**maïs** *(meh-eez)*

cow *(kahu)*　**vache** *(vahsh)*

cowboy
(cahu-bohi)

cow-boy
(coh-oo/boo-ah)

crab *(crab)*　**crabe** *(crahb)*

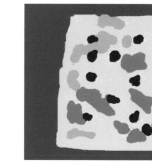

cracker
(cra-ker)

craquelin
(crahc-lah)

crib
(crib)

berceau
(behr-soo)

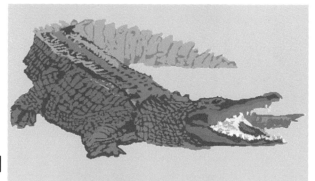

crocodile *(cro-ca-drol)*
crocodile *(croh-coh-dree-leh)*

C

cross *(cross)*   croix *(croo-ah)*

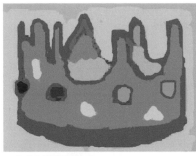

crown
(crah-oun)

couronne *(coh-rohn)*

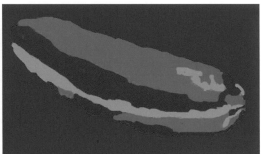

cucumber *(kiu-cum-ber)*
concombre *(coh-coombr)*

cup
(cap)

tasse
(tahss)

D

daisy
(dei-si)

marguerite
(mahr-geh-reet)

deer *(dii-ehr)*   cerfs *(cehrg)*

desk
(desk)

bureau *(bee-oo-roh)*

dice
(da-iis)

dé
(deh)

18

D

disk
(disk)

disque
(deesk)

doctor
(doc-tor)

docteur
(dohc-tehr)

dog
(dog)

chien
(shee-eean)

doll
(dohll)

poupée
(poo-peh)

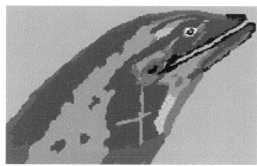

dolphin
(dol-fihn)

dauphin
(doh-phah)

domino *(do-mi-no)*
domino *(doh-mee-noh)*

donkey
(don-qui)

âne *(ahn)*

door
(door)

porte
(pohrt)

19

D

dragon *(dra-gon)*   dragon *(drah-gohn)*

dress *(dress)*

robe *(rohb)*

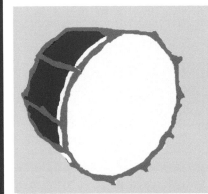

drum *(drom)*

tambour *(tahm-boor)*

duck *(dack)*

canard *(cah-nahr)*

E

eagle *(i-gol)*   aigle *(ah-ee-glah)*

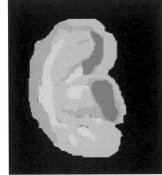

ear *(i-ahr)*

oreille *(oh-reh-eel)*

earphone *(ir-fon)*
écouteur *(eh-coo-tehr)*

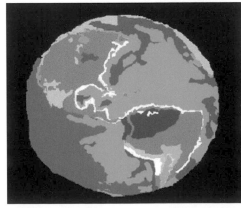

earth *(erth)*

terre *(tehrr)*

20

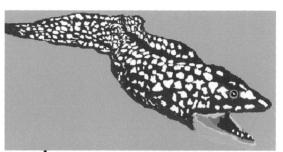

eel *(i-ohl)*   anguille *(ahn-geel)*

E

egg *(egg)*   oeuf *(oh-ooph)*

eggplant *(egg-plahnth)*
aubergine *(oh-behr-sheen)*

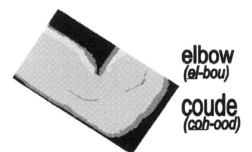

elbow
(el-bou)

coude
(cob-ood)

elephant
(e-le-fanth)

éléphant *(eh-leh-phan)*

elevator
(eh-leh-vei-ror)

ascenseur
(ahs-cehn-sehr)

elk *(elk)*   élan *(eh-lohn)*

engineer
(ehn-shi-niehr)

ingénieur *(ahn-she-nee-ehr)*

envelope *(ehn-ve-lohp)*
envelopper *(ahn-veh-lo-peh)*

E

escalator *(ehç-ca-leh-i-ror)*
escalator *(ehs-keh-lah-tohr)*

eskimo *(ehç-ki-mo)*
esquimau *(ehs-kee-moh)*

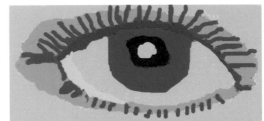

eye *(ah-ih)*

oeil *(oh-eel)*

F

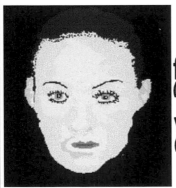

face *(feh-ihç)*

visage *(vee-sash)*

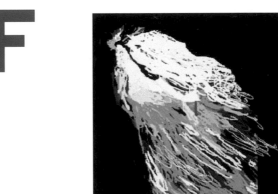

fairy *(fe-ri)*

fée *(fee)*

falcon *(fal-con)*

faucon *(phoo-cohn)*

fan *(fehn)*

ventilateur *(vehn-tee-lah-tehr)*

22

farm *(farm)*   ferme *(fehrm)*

faucet *(fo-cet)*

robinet *(roh-bee-neh)*

feather *(feh-der)*

plume *(plee-oom)*

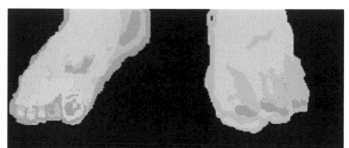

feet *(fiith)*   pieds *(pee-eh)*

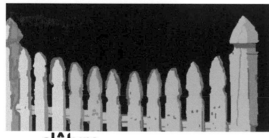

fence *(fenç)*

clôture *(cloh-tee-oor)*

fern *(fern)*

fougère *(foo-shehr)*

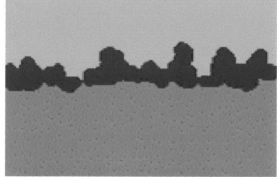

field *(fi-old)*   champ *(shahmp)*

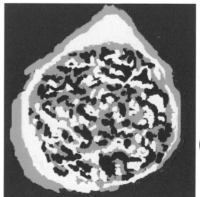

fig *(fig)*

fico *(fee-coh)*

23

F

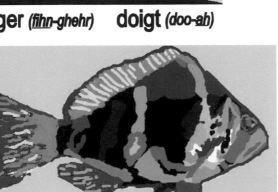

finger *(fihn-ghehr)*   **doigt** *(doo-ah)*

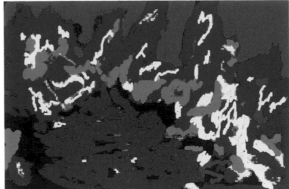

fire *(fa-ior)*   **feu** *(fehg)*

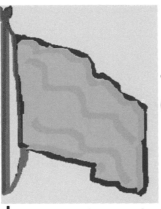

fish *(fish)*   **poisson** *(poo-eh-sohn)*

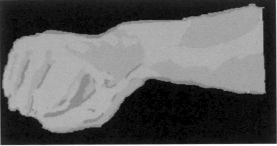

fist *(fist)*   **poing** *(poo-ahng)*

flag *(flag)*

drapeau *(drah-poh)*

flamingo *(fla-min-go)*

flamant *(flah-moh)*

flashlight *(flash-lahith)*

lampe de poche *(lahmp/deh/pohsh)*

flower *(fla-uer)*

fleur *(flehr)*

24

F

fly *(flahi)* mouche *(moh-oosh)*

forest *(fo-resth)*

forêt *(foh-reh)*

fork *(fork)*

fourchette *(foor-sheht)*

fox *(fox)*

renard *(reh-nahr)*

frame *(freiihm)* cadre *(cadr)*

frog *(frog)*

grenouille *(grah-noo-lleh)*

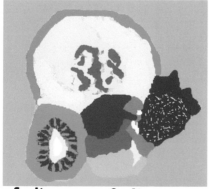

fruit *(fruth)* fruit *(phroo-ee)*

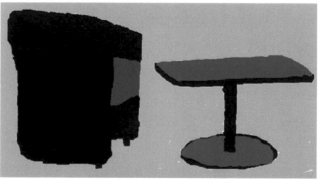

furniture *(for-ni-chur)*
meubles *(meh-oo-bleh)*

25

G

garage *(ga-rash)*
garage *(gah-rash)*

garlic
(gar-lic)

ail
(ah-eel)

gazelle *(ga-zel)* **gazelle** *(gah-zehl)*

gift
(ghifth)

cadeau
(cah-doo)

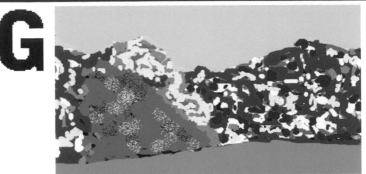

garden *(gar-dehn)*   **jardin** *(shahr-dehn)*

gate *(ghehith)*   **porte** *(pohrt)*

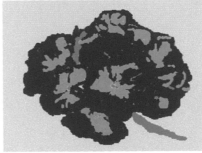

geranium
(sheh-re-nium)

géranium
(sheh-rah-nee-oom)

giraffe
(shi-raf)

girafe
(she-raph)

26

G

gladiolus
(gla-die-los)

gladioulus
(glah-dee-oh-lee)

glasses
(gla-seç)

verres *(vehrr)*

globe
(glob)

globe
(glohb)

glove
(glouv)

gant
(gohn)

goat *(go-uth)*   chèvre *(shehvr)*

goblet
(ga-bleth)

verre à pied
(vehrr/ah/pee-ehd)

goose *(guç)*   oie *(oo-ah)*

grapes *(greipç)*   raisins *(reh-sahn)*

27

G

grass *(graç)*   **herbe** *(ehrb)*

grasshopper *(gras-oh-per)*
sauterelle *(soo-trehl)*

guitar
(ghi-tar)

guitare
(gee-tahr)

gull
(goh-ul)

mouette
(moo-eht)

H

ham *('ham)*   **jambon** *(shahm-boh)*

hamburger *('ham-bur-guer)*
hamburger *(hahm-boor-gehr)*

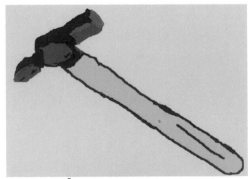

hammer *('ha-mer)*
marteau *(mahr-too)*

hammock *('ha-mek)*
hamac *(ah-mahk)*

28

H

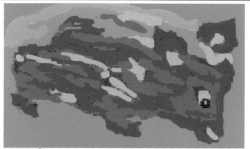

hamster *(hams-ter)*
hamster *(ahms-tehr)*

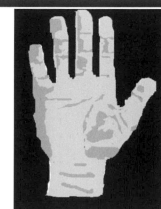

hand *('hahnd)*

main *(mah)*

handbag *('hand-bahg)*

sac à main *(sahk/ah/mah)*

handkerchief *('hahnd-ker-kif)*

mouchoir *(moo-shoo-ah)*

hare *('her)*

lièvre *(lee-ehvr)*

harp *('harp)*

harpe *(ahrp)*

hat *('hath)*

chapeau *(shah-poo)*

hawk *('hak)*   **faucon** *(phob-coh)*

29

H

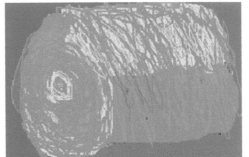

hay ('he-ii)   foin (phoo-ah)

head ("hed)

tête (teht)

heart ('harth)

coeur (kegr)

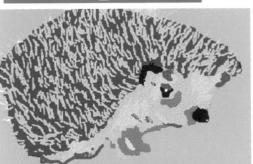

hedgehog ('hedsh-'hog)
hérisson (eh-ree-sohn)

helmet ('hel-meth)

casque (cahsk)

hen ('hehn)

poule (pooll)

highway ('hah-ii-goo-eh-ii)
route nationale
(roogt/nah-see-oh-nahl)

hoe ('ho-oo)

houe (oh-oo)

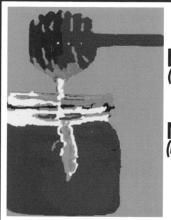

honey
('ha-ni)

miel
(mee-ehl)

H

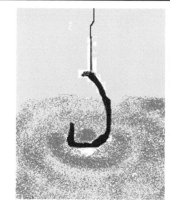

hook
('huk)

agrafe
(ah-grahph)

horn *('horn)*   **corne** *(cohgm)*

horse
('horss)

cheval
(sheh-vahl)

horseshoe
('hors-shu)

fer à cheval
(fehr-ah-sheh-vahl)

hourglass
(aur-glas)

sablier
(sah-blee-ehr)

hydrant
('ha-ii-drahnth)

prise d'eau
(prees-d'oo)

house *('ha-us)*
maison *(meh-sohn)*

31

ice cream
(ah-iiç/crim)

glace
(glahss)

I

ice cubes
(aiiç-kiubç)

cubes de glace *(coob/doo/glahs)*

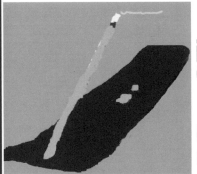

ice skates
(ais-skeitç)

patins
(pah-tehn)

igloo
(ah-ii-gloo)

igloo
(ee-gloo)

incense
(ii-ncéénss)

encens
(ohn-sah)

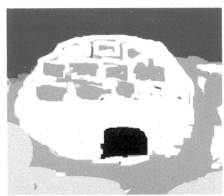

iris
(ah-ii-riiç)

iris
(ee-rees)

iron
(ah-ii-ron)

fer *(fehr)*

island *(ah-ii-lahnd)*   île *(eel)*

J

jack in the box
(shack/in/deh/box)

cric dans la boîte
(cree/dohn/lah/boo-aht)

jackal *(sha-kol)*   **chacal** *(shah-kahl)*

jacket
(shah-keth)

jaquette
(shah-keht)

jaguar *(sha-guar)*
jaguar *(sha-gooar)*

jail
(sheil)

prison
(pree-sohn)

jam
(sham)

confiture
(cohn-phee-tee-oor)

jar
(shar)

jarre
(shagr)

jasmine
(shahç-meen)

jazmin *(shahs-mah)*

33

J

jeans
(shihnç)

jean
(shoh)

jelly beans
(she-li/bihnç)

haricots de gelée
(ah-ree-coh/deh/sheh-leh)

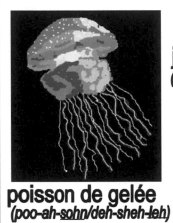

jelly fish
(sheh-li/fish)

poisson de gelée
(poo-ah-sohn/deh-sheh-leh)

jig-saw puzzle
*(zig/saoo/
zig/saoo/pá-zol)*

remuez le puzzle d'affaissement
(reh-mee-ooeh/leh/pozz/dah-fees-mah)

jug
(shog)

cruche
(croosh)

jockey
(sho-ki)

jockey
(shoh-keh)

juice
(shuç)

jus
(shoo)

jungle *(shan-gol)*
jungle *(shahngl)*

K

kangaroo *(kehn-ghe-roo)*
kangourou *(kahn-goh-roo)*

karate *(ka-ra-ri)*

karaté *(kah-rah-teh)*

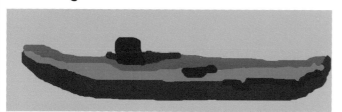

kayak *(ka-iac)*   **kayac** *(keh-yahc)*

kennel *(ke-nol)*
chenil *(sheh-neel)*

ketchup *(keth-chop)*

ketchup *(keht-choop)*

KETCHUP

kettle *(ke-rol)*

bouilloire *(boh-ool-ee-ahr)*

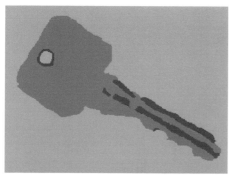

key *(kii)*   **clé** *(clee)*

kite *(ka-ith)*

cerf-volant *(cehr/voo-loh)*

K

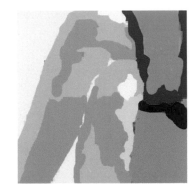

knees
(kniiç)

genoux
(sheh-noo)

kitten *(ki-rehn)* chaton *(shah-toh)*

knife
(knah-iif)

couteau
(coo-toh)

koala bear
(koh-ah-lah/ber)

ours de koala
(oors/deh/koo-eh-lah)

L

labyrinth *(la-ba-riiith)*
labyrinthe *(lah-bee-rahnt)*

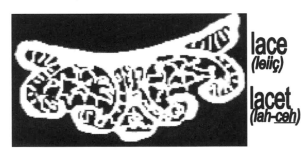

lace
(leiiç)

lacet
(lah-ceh)

ladder
(lah-der)

échelle
(eh-shehl)

ladybug
(lei-di-bog)

coccinelle
(cohc-zee-nehl)

L

lamb *(lahmb)*   **agneau** *(ahg-nee-oo)*

lamp *(lahmp)*

lampe *(lohm)*

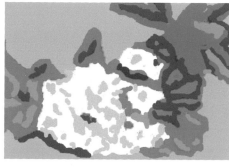

laurel *(lohu-rol)*

laurier *(loh-ree-eh)*

lavender *(leh-ii-vahn-der)*

lavande *(lah-voh)*

lawn mower *(lan/moh-er)*

tondeuse à gazon *(toon-dehs/ah/gah-zohn)*

leaf *(lif)*

feuille *(pheh-ee-eh)*

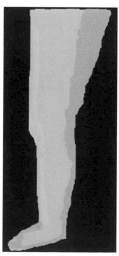

leg *(leg)*

jambe *(shamb)*

lemon *(le-mon)*

citron *(see-troh)*

37

L

leopard
(le-perd)

léopard
(leh-oh-pahr)

lettuce
(le-rooç)

laitue
(leh-too)

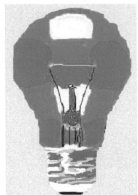

lightbulb
(la-ith-bolb)

ampoule
(ahm-pool)

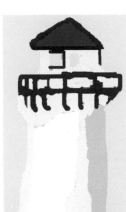

lighthouse
(la-ith-'ha-hus)

phare
(phah)

lilac
(lah-ii-lac)

lilas
(lee-lah)

lime
(lah-iim)

tilleul
(tee-lee-ohl)

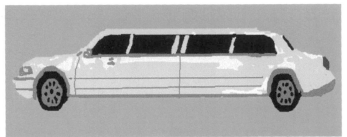

limousine *(li-mu-sin)*   limousine *(lee-moh-seen)*

lion
(la-ion)

lion
(lee-oh)

38

lips *(li-ps)*

lèvres *(lehvr)*

L

lizard *(li-zard)*   **lézard** *(lízahrd)*

lobster *(lobss-ter)*

homard *(oh-mahs)*

lock *(lock)*

serrure *(seh-rroor)*

lollipop *(lo-li-pop)*

sucette *(she-oo-ceht)*

lovebirds *(lov-berdç)*

perruches inséparables
(peh-roo-shehg/ehn-see-pah-rah-ble)

luggage *(lo-ghéch)*
bagages *(bah-gahsh)*

lynx *(líhnkzç)*

lynx *(lahnxz)*

M

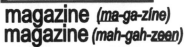

magazine *(ma-ga-zíne)*
magazine *(mah-gah-zeen)*

magician *(ma-gi-shian)*

magicien *(mah-she-see-ah)*

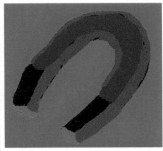

magnet *(mag-neth)*

aimant *(eh-mohn)*

magnolia *(mag-no-li-a)*

magnolia *(mah-nee-oh-lee-ah)*

maid *(mehídh)*

bonne *(bohn)*

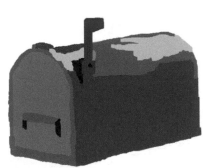

mailbox *(mail-box)*

boîte aux lettres *(boo-aht/oo/letg)*

mammoth *(me-moç)*
mammouth *(mah-moot)*

mandarin *(mehn-da-rihn)*
mandarine *(mohn-dah-reen)*

40

M

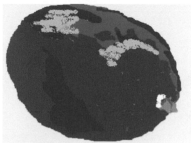

mango *(meh-iihn-go)*
mangue *(mohng)*

map *(map)*   **carte** *(cahrt)*

maple leaf *(mei-pol/lif)*
feuille d'érable
(pheh-eeoo/deh/rabl)

marigold *(me-ri-gold)*

souci *(soh-see)*

mask *(mask)*

masque *(mahsk)*

matchbox *(mhatsh-box)*

boîte d'allumettes
(boo-aht/d'/ah-loo-meht)

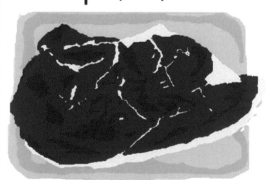

meat *(mith)*   **viande** *(vee-ahnd)*

medal *(me-dal)*

médaille *(meh-dah-il)*

41

M

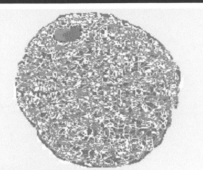

melon *(me-lohn)*
melon *(meh-loh)*

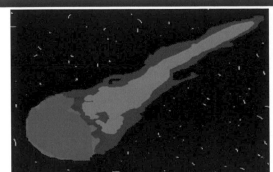

meteor *(mi-ri-or)*
météore *(mee-teh-ohr)*

milk *(milk)*

lait *(leh)*

mirror *(mi-ror)*

miroir *(mee-rroo-ah)*

mitten *(mitn)*

moufle *(moofl)*

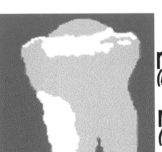

molar *(mohu-ler)*

molaire *(moh-lehr)*

mole *(moul)*　**taupe** *(tohp)*

money *(ma-ni)*　**argent** *(ahr-shon)*

monitor *(mo-ni-rer)*
moniteur *(moh-nee-tehr)*

monkey *(mohn-ki)*

singe *(sahnsh)*

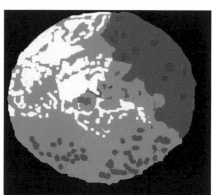

moon *(moohn)* **lune** *(lloonn)*

mountain *(moun-tehn)*
montagne *(mohn-tahg-nee-ah)*

mouse *(mahooss)* **souris** *(soo-ree)*

moustache *(mosh-tesh)* **moustache** *(moos-tash)*

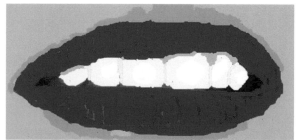

mouth *(mauz)* **bouche** *(boosh)*

mushroom
(mash-rrum)

champignon
(shahm-pee-nee-ohn)

43

nail
(neh-il)

ongle
(oongl)

N

napkins *(nap-kinç)*
serviettes *(sehr-vee-ehts)*

neck *(neck)*   cou *(coo)*

necklace
(neck-leis)

collier
(coh-lle-eh)

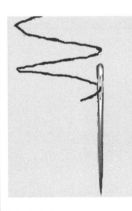

needle
(ni-rol)

aiguille
(eh-goo-ee-ah)

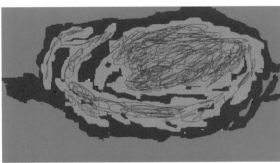

nest
(nesth)

nid
(nee)

newspaper *(niuss-pei-per)*
journal *(shohr-nahl)*

nightingale
(nahii-tiihn-ghel)

rossignol
(roh-see-nee-ohl)

44

N

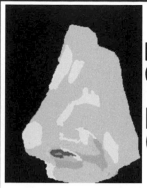

nose
(nohuç)

nez
(neh)

nutcracker
(nath-krah-ker)

casse-noix
(cass/noh-ah)

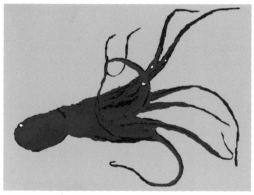

notebook *(nouth-book)*
carnet *(cahr-neh)*

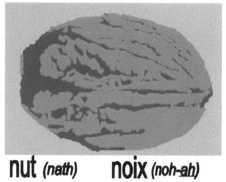

nut *(nath)*   noix *(noh-ah)*

O

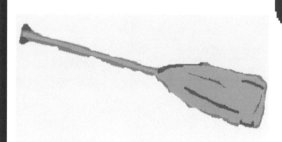

oar *(oiiar)*   rame *(rahm)*

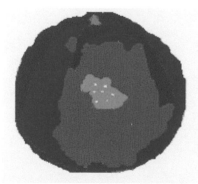

octopus *(oc-tuh-puhç)*
pieuvre *(pee-ehvr)*

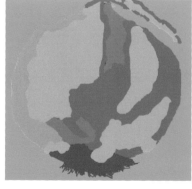

onion
(o-ni-ohn)

oignon
(ohg-nee-ohn)

orange
(o-ransh)

orange
(ohg-rahnsh)

O

orchid
(or-quid)

orchidée *(ohr-kee-dee)*

ostrich
(os-trich)

autruche
(oh-troosh)

owl
(ah-ul)

hibou
(ee-boo)

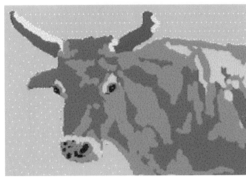

OX
(ox)

bœuf
(behff)

P

paint
(peh-iinth)

peinture
(peh-een-toor)

palm
(palm)

paume
(pahgm)

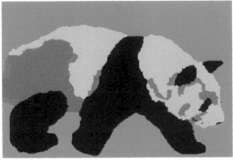

panda
(pan-da)

panda
(pohn-dah)

pansy
(pehn-si)

pensée
(pohn-see)

P

panther *(pan-ter)*   panthère *(pahn-tehgr)*

parachute *(per-a-shuth)*

parachute *(pah-rah-shoot)*

parakeet *(per-kith)*

perruche *(pehg-rroosh)*

parasol *(per-a-sol)*

ombrelle *(ohm-brehl)*

parrot *(pe-rroth)*

perroquet *(peh-rroh-keh)*

parsley *(pars-li)*

persil *(pehr-see)*

passport *(pass-port)*

passeport *(pahss-pohr)*

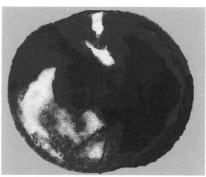

peach *(pich)*

pêche *(pehsh)*

47

P

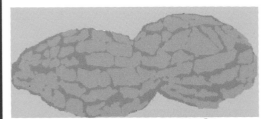

peanut*(pi-nath)* cacahuète *(cah-cah-oo-eht)*

pear
(peerr)

poire
(poo-ahr)

pecan
(pi-ken)

noix de pecan
(noo-ah/dee/pee-cahn)

pelican
(pe-li-cahn)

pélican
(peh-lee-cohn)

pen
(pehn)

stylo
(stee-loh)

pencil
(pehn-sol)

crayon
(creh-ee-ohn)

penguin
(pehn-guh-iihn)

pingouin
(pehn-goo-ah)

piano
(pia-no)

piano *(pee-ah-noh)*

P

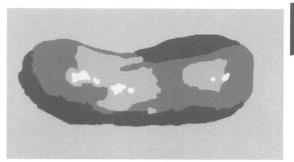

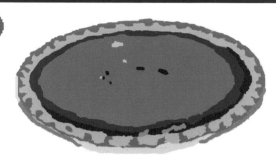

pickle *(pi-col)*   pickles *(pee-kehls)*

pie *(pahi)*   tourte *(too-ohrt)*

pig *(pig)*   cochon *(coh-shohn)*

pigeon *(pi-shih-on)*   pigeon *(pee-shohn)*

pillow
(pi-lou)

oreiller
(oh-rehg-ee-eh)

pin
(piihn)

épingle
(eh-pah-glah)

pine
(pa-iihn)

pin
(pah)

pineapple
(pa-in-a-pol)

ananas
(ah-nah-nah)

49

P

pinecone
(pah-iihn-cohn)

pomme de pin *(pohm/deh/pah)*

pitcher
(pith-cher)

pichet
(pee-sheh)

plate *(pleiith)*   **assiette** *(ah-see-eht)*

platypus   *(pla-ri-puss)*
platypus   *(plah-tee-poo)*

plum
(plam)

prune *(proonn)*

polar bear
(po-lar/beerr)

ours polaire *(oors/poo-lehr)*

pony
(po-nii)

poney
(poo-neh)

pot *(poth)*   **pot** *(poh)*

50

P

potato *(po-teii-ro)*
pomme de terre *(pohm/deh/tehrr)*

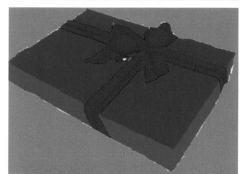

present *(préh-sénth)*
présent *(preh-sohn)*

pumpkin
(pahmp-kiihn)

citrouille
(see-troh-ool)

puppy
(pa-pl)

chiot
(she-oh)

Q

quail
(cuel)

caille
(cah-eel)

quarter
(cuh-oh-ra)

quart de dollar
(cahrt/deh/doh-llahr)

queen
(quh-iihn)

reine *(reh-een)*

quince
(cuh-iihnç)

coing
(coo-ah)

51

R

raccoon *(ra-coohn)*

raccon *(rah-coo)*

rabbit *(ra-bith)*
lapin *(lah-pah)*

racket *(ra-queth)*

raquette *(rah-keht)*

radio *(rei-dio)*

radio *(rah-dee-oh)*

radish *(ra-dish)*   **radis** *(rah-dee)*

rainbow *(reh-iihn-bou)*   arc-en-ciel *(ahrk/ehn/see-ehl)*

rake *(reiik)*

ratisser *(rah-tee-seh)*

raspberry *(rasp-beh-rri)*
framboise *(frahm-boo-ehs)*

52

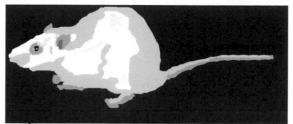

rat *(rath)* rat *(rah)*

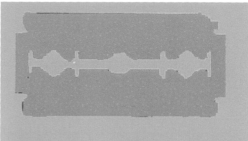

razor *(reii-zor)* rasoir *(reh-soo-ah)*

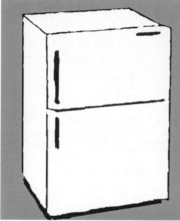

refrigerator
(re-fri-shi-reii-rohr)

réfrigérateur
(reh-phree-sheh-rah-tohr)

reindeer *(reiihn-diiehr)* renne *(rehn)*

rhinoceros *(rai-no-ceh-rehç)*
rhinocéros *(ree-noh-ceh-rohs)*

ribbon
(ri-bon)

cordon
(cohrg-dohn)

robot
(ruh-both)

robot
(roh-boh)

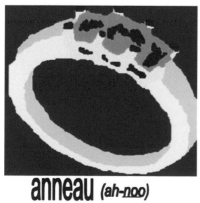

ring
(niihngh)

anneau *(ah-noo)*

R

53

R

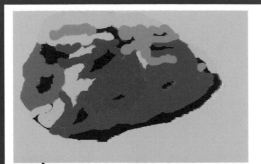

rock *(rock)*   roche *(rohsh)*

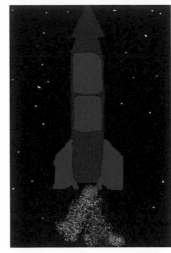

rocket
(ro-keth)

fusée
(phee-oo-seh)

roof *(ruf)*   toit *(too-ah)*

rooster
(ruç-ter)

coq
(cohk)

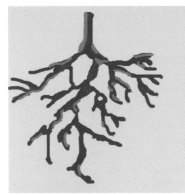

root
(ruth)

racine
(rah-seenn)

rope
(rohup)

corde
(cohgrd)

rose
(roh-us)

rose
(rohgs)

ruler *(ru-ler)*
règle *(reh-gl)*

54

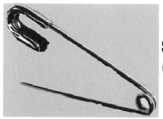

safety pin
(seif-ti/piihn)

S

salamander *(sal-a-mehn-der)*
salamandre *(sah-lah-mahndr)*

sandal *(sahn-dal)*
sandale *(sohn-dahl)*

sausage *(so-sesh)*
saucisse *(soh-sees)*

épingle de sûreté
(eh-pahn-gl/doh/see-oor-teh)

school
(scul)

école
(eh-cohl)

scale *(skel)*
échelle *(eh-shehl)*

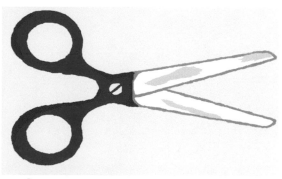

scooter
(scu-rer)

scissors *(si-sorç)*
ciseaux *(see-soh)*

scooter *(scoo-tehr)*

55

S

scorpion *(scor-pion)*
scorpion *(scohr-pee-ohn)*

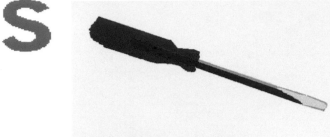

screwdriver *(scru-drah-ii-ver)*
tournevis *(tohr-neh-vees)*

sea lion *(si/la-ion)*
lion marin *(lee-ohn/mah-rah)*

seagull *(si-gul)*

mouette *(moo-eht)*

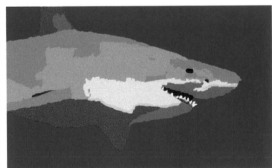

shark *(shark)*   aigrefin *(a-groo-phah)*

sheep *(ship)*

moutons *(moo-tohn)*

shell *(shell)*

coquille *(coh-kee-ah)*

ship *(ship)*   navire *(nah-vee-ahr)*

56

shirt
(sherth)

chemise
(cheh-<u>meez</u>)

S

shoe *(shu)*
chaussure *(<u>shoh</u>-see-oor)*

shorts *(shortss)*   short *(shohrt)*

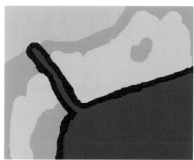

shoulder
(<u>shohul</u>-der)

épaule
(<u>eh</u>-poh-ool)

shovel
(sha-vol)

pelle
(pehll)

shower
(<u>sha</u>-goo-er)

douche
(doosh)

shrimp
(shriimp)

crevette
(creh-<u>veht</u>)

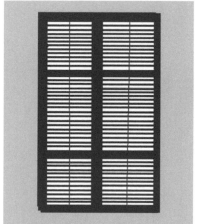

shutter
(sha-rer)

volet *(voh-leh)*

57

S

skillet *(ski-leth)*   **poêle** *(poh-ehl)*

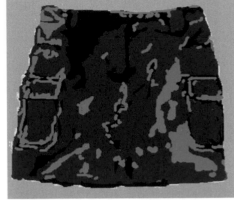

skirt *(skerth)*   **jupe** *(shoop)*

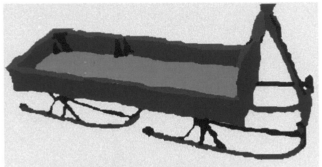

sled *(sledh)*   **luge** *(loogsh)*

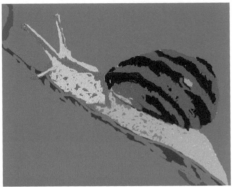

snail *(sneil)*   **escargot** *(ehs-cahr-goh)*

snake *(sneiik)*

serpent *(sehr-pohn)*

snow *(snou)*

neige *(nehsh)*

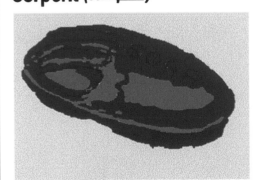

soap *(sohup)*

savon *(sah-vohn)*

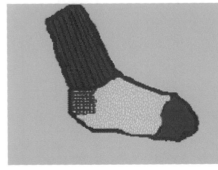

sock *(sock)*

chaussette *(shoh-oo-seht)*

S

sofa (*sohu-fa*)   sofa (*soh-phah*)

sparrow
(*spe-rrou*)

moineau
(*moo-eh-noo*)

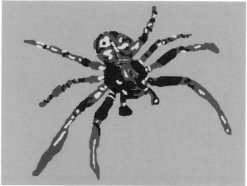

spider (*speii-der*)
araignée (*ah-rahg-nee-eh*)

spiderweb
(*speii-der-web*)

toile d'araignée
(*too-ehl/dah-rag-nee-eh*)

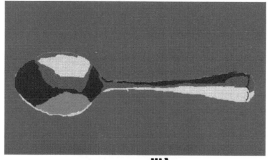

spoon (*spoon*)   cuillère (*coo-lee-ehr*)

squirrel
(*scuerl*)

écureuil (*eh-coo-roh-eel*)

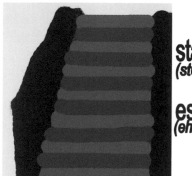

stair
(*ster*)

escalier
(*ehs-cah-lee-eh*)

stamp
(*stamp*)

cachet
(*cah-sheh*)

59

S

starfish
(star-fish)

étoile de mer
(eh-too-ehl/deh/mehr)

stork
(stork)

cigogne *(see-goh-nee-eh)*

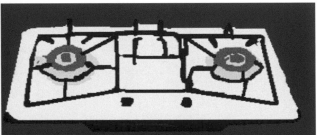

stove *(stouv)*   cuisinière *(coo-see-nee-ehr)*

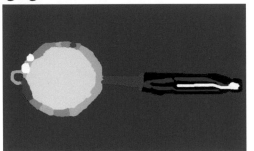

strainer *(stri-ner)*
passoire *(pah-ee-soo-ah)*

strawberry
(stro-beh-rri)

fraise
(phreh-sah)

sun
(sahn)

soleil
(soh-leh-eel)

sunflower
(sahn-fla-uerr)

tournesol
(toor-neh-sohl)

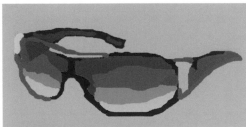

sunglasses *(san-gla-ses)*
lunettes de soleil
(loo-neht/deh/soh/lee-ehl)

60

S

surf-board
(sorf-bord)

planche de surf
(plahnsh/deh/sehrf)

sweater *(sueh-rer)*
chandail *(sahn-dahl)*

T

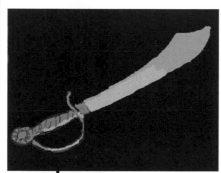

sword *(suordh)*
épée *(eh-peh)*

table
(tei-bol)

table
(tah-blah)

teapot *(tii-poth)*   théière *(teh-ee-ehr)*

telephone
(te-le-fon)

téléphone
(teh-leh-phohn)

telescope
(te-less-cop)

télescope
(teh-lehs-cohp)

television
(te-le-vi-shion)

télévision *(teh-leh-vee-shee-ohn)*

61

T

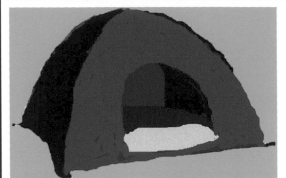

tent *(tehnth)* tente *(tohnt)*

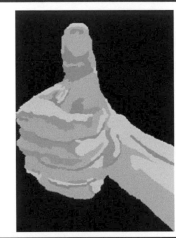

thumb *(zahm)*

pouce *(pooss)*

tie *(taii)*

cravate *(crah-yaht)*

tiger *(tai-gher)*

tigre *(tee-gr)*

toaster *(tous-ter)*

toasteur *(toos-tehr)*

tomato *(to-mehii-ro)*

tomate *(toh-maht)*

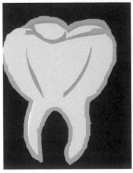

tooth *(tuz)*

dent *(dohn)*

torch *(torch)*

torche *(tohrsh)*

T

toucan
(tu-ken)

toucan
(too-cohn)

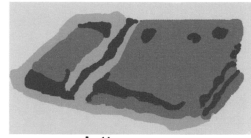

towel
(ta-uel)

serviette *(sehr-vee-eht)*

tower
(tah-uehr)

tour
(toor)

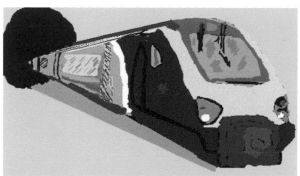

train
(tré-iin)

train
(trahn)

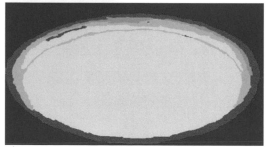

tray *(trei)*   plateau *(plah-toh)*

tree
(tri)

arbre
(ahrb)

truck *(track)*   camion *(cah-mee-ohn)*

trumpet *(trom-peth)*
trompette *(troo-peht)*

63

T

tulip
(tu-lipe)

tulipe
(choo-leep)

tunnel *(ta-nol)*   tunnel *(too-nehl)*

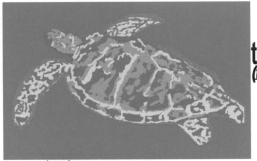

turtle
(to-rrol)

tortue *(tohr-too)*

U

umbrella
(am-bréh-la)

parapluie
(pah-rah-plee)

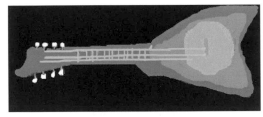

ukulele *(io-ko-leh-leh)*
guitare hawaïenne
(gee-tahr/ah-ee-ehn)

uphill
(ap-hil)

montée *(mohn-teh)*

u turn
(iu-torn)

u-tour
(ee-oo/toor)

64

V

valve *(valve)*   valve *(vahlv)*

vase
(veiiç)

vase
(vahs)

vest *(vesth)* *(sho-leh)* gilet

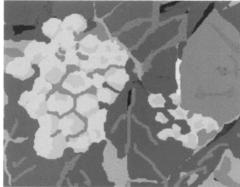

vine
(va-iinn)

vigne
(veeg-nee-eh)

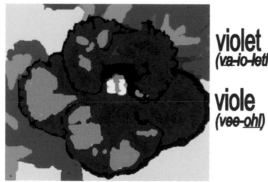

violet
(va-io-leth)

viole
(vee-ohl)

violin
(va-io-liihn)

violon
(vee-oh-lohn)

visor *(vahii-sor)*   visière *(vee-see-ehr)*

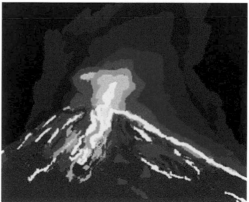

volcano
(vol-keii-no)

volcan
(vohl-cahn)

65

W

waffle *(ua-fol)*
gaufre *(gohfr)*

wagon *(ua-gon)*

chariot *(shah-ree-oh)*

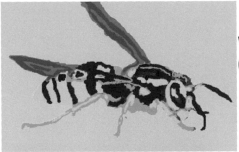

walkie-talkie *(ua-kii/tol-kii)*

walkie-film-parlant *(vahl-kee/pheelm/pahr-lohn)*

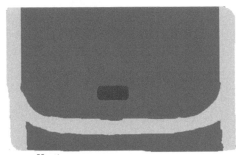

wallet *(wa-let)*
portefeuille *(pohr-teh-pheh-eel)*

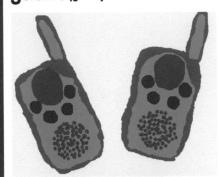

wasp *(guasp)*

guêpe *(gehp)*

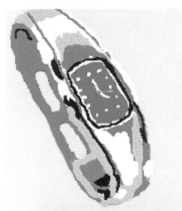

watch *(guatch)*

montre *(mohntr)*

waterfall *(gua-der-fol)*

cascade *(cahs-cahd)*

watering can *(gua-de-riing/cahn)*
arrosoir *(ah-rroh-soo-ah)*

66

W

watermelon *(gua-der-meh-lohn)*
pastèque *(pahs-tehk)*

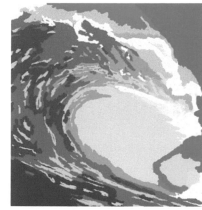

wave
(uehiiv)

vague
(vahg)

weather vane
(gue-der/veh-iihn)

girouette météorologique
(she-oo-reht/meh-teh-oh-roh-loh-sheek)

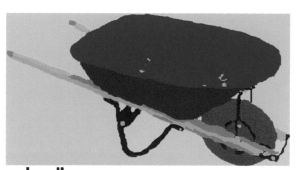

whale *(guel)*   **baleine** *(bah-leh-een)*

wheel
(ui-ol)

roue
(roo)

wheelbarrow *(guiol-ba-rrou)*
brouette *(broo-eht)*

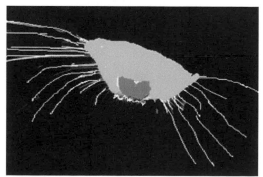

whiskers *(uiss-kerç)*
moustaches *(moos-tahsh)*

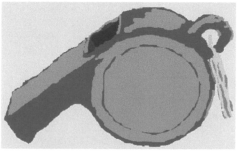

whistle
(ui-sol)

sifflet *(see-pleh)*

67

W

wig *(uiig)* perruque *(peh-rook)*

window *(u-iin-dou)*

fenêtre *(pheh-nehtr)*

wings *(uiinngç)* ailes *(ehl)*

wolf *(wuf)*

loup *(loo)*

wood *(wudh)* bois *(boo-ah)*

wool *(wul)*

laine *(lehn)*

worm *(uorm)* ver *(vehr)*

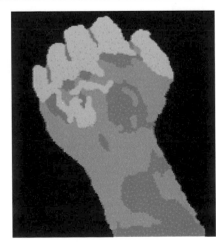

wrist *(rist)*

poignet *(pohg-nee-eh)*

X

X- mas
(*criss-maç*)

Noël
(*noh-ehl*)

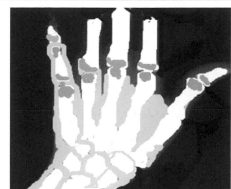

X- ray (*ex-reii*)
Rayons X (*rah-ee-ohn/dees*)

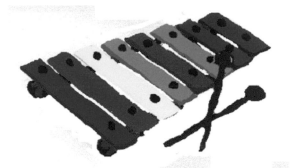

xylophone (*zahii-lo-fon*)
xylophone (*see-loh-phohn*)

Y

yacht (*iiahth*)   yacht (*ee-oht*)

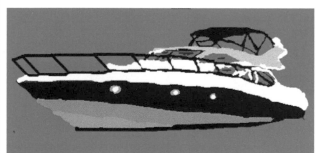

yam (*iiam*)   patate (*pah-taht*)

yield
(*iieldh*)

céder
(*ceh-deh*)

yogurt
(*io-gurth*)

yogourt
(*ee-oh-goor*)

69

Z

zebra *(zi-bra)*   **zèbre** *(zehbr)*

zebu *(zi-bu)*   **zebu** *(zeh-booh)*

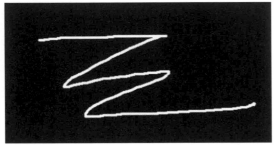

zipper *(zi-per)*

zigzag *(zig-zag)*   **zigzag** *(zeeg-zahg)*

fermeture éclair *(fehr-meh-toohr/eh-clehr)*

A

abeille *(ah-beh-ee-lleh)* bee *(bi)*

aéroplane *(ah-eh-roh-plahn)* airplane *(eir-plihn)*

agneau *(ahg-nee-oo)* lamb *(lahmb)*

agrafe *(ah-grahph)* hook *('huk)*

aigle *(ah-ee-glah)* eagle *(i-gol)*

aigrefin *(a-groo-phah)* shark *(shark)*

aiguille *(eh-goo-ee-ah)* needle *(ni-rol)*

ail *(ah-eel)* garlic *(gar-lic)*

ailes *(ehl)* wings *(uiinngç)*

aimant *(eh-mohn)* magnet *(mag-neth)*

alligator *(ah-lee-gah-toh-h)* alligator *(a-li-ghei-ror)*

ambulance *(ahm-boo-lohns)* ambulance *(am-bhiu-lahnç)*

ampoule *(ahm-pool)* lightbulb *(la-ith-bolb)*

ananas *(ah-nah-nah)* pineapple *(pain-a-pol)*

âne *(ahn)* donkey *(don-ki)*

ange *(ohnsh)* angel *(ewhn-shol)*

anguille *(ahn-geel)* eel *(i-ohl)*

anneau *(ah-noo)* ring *(riihngh)*

appareil de photo *(ah-pah-rehl/deh/phoh-toh)* camera *(ca-me-ra)*

appartement *(ah-pahg-tah-meh)* apartment *(a-parth-menth)*

aquarium *(ah-coo-ah-ree-om)* aquarium *(a-cue-rium)*

araignée *(ah-rahg-nee-eh)* spider *(speii-der)*

arbre *(ahrb)* tree *(tri)*

arc *(ahrk)* arc *(arc)*

arc-en-ciel *(ahrk/ehn/see-ehl)* rainbow *(reh-iihn-bou)*

arche *(ahrsh)* ark *(ark)*

argent *(ahr-shon)* money *(ma-ni)*

arrosoir *(ah-rroh-soo-ah)* watering can *(gua-de-riing/cahn)*

ascenseur *(ahs-cehn-sehr)* elevator *(eh-leh-vei-ror)*

assiette *(ah-see-eht)* plate *(pleiith)*

athlète *(ah-tleht)* athlete *(a-tlihth)*

aubergine *(oh-behr-sheen)* eggplant *(egg-plahnth)*

automne *(oo-tohm)* autumn *(o-rom)*

automobile *(oo-too-moh-bee-lah)* automobile *(ah-ro-mo-bil)*

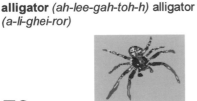

bagages (*bah-gahsh*) luggage (*lo-ghéch*)

balai (*bah-leh*) broom (*broum*)

ballet (*bah-ee-leh*) ballet (*ba-leth*)

ballon (*bah-loo*) balloon (*ba-loun*)

banane (*bah-nah-nah*) banana (*ba-na-na*)

banc (*boh*) bench (*behnch*)

bandage (*boh-dahsh*) bandage (*bahn-detch*)

barbecue (*bahr-beh-koo*) barbecue (*bar-bi-quiu*)

bateau (*bah-too*) boat (*bout*)

batterie (*bah-tree*) battery (*ba-re-ri*)

bébé (*beh-beh*) baby (*bei-bi*)

berceau (*behr-soo*) crib (*crib*)

beurre (*behgr*) butter (*ba-rer*)

B

bicyclette (*bee-see-cleht*) bicycle (*bahi-si-col*)

binoculaires (*bee-noh-kee-oo-lehr*) binoculars (*bahi-no-quiu-lahrç*)

biscuit (*bees-kee-oo*) biscuit (*bis-ket*)

bison (*bee-zohn*) bison (*bahi-son*)

bœuf (*behff*) ox (*ox*)

bois (*boo-ah*) wood (*wudh*)

boite (*boo-aht*) can (*quen*)

boîte aux lettres (*boo-aht/oo/letg*) mailbox (*meil-box*)

boîte d'allumettes (*boo-aht/d'/ah-loo-meht*) matchbox (*match-box*)

bonbon (*bohn-bohn*) candy (*khen-di*)

bonne (*bohn*) maid (*mehídh*)

botte (*boht*) boot (*boot*)

bouche (*boosh*) mouth (*maooz*)

bouilloire (*boh-ool-ee-ahr*) kettle (*ke-rol*)

bouquet (*boo-keh*) bouquet (*bou-ke*)

bouteille (*boh-oo-teh-ee-eh*) bottle (*ba-rol*)

bracelet (*brahz-leht*) bracelet (*braeh-ihss-leth*)

bras (*brah*) arm (*arm*)

briques (*breek*) bricks (*brickç*)

broccoli (*broh-coh-lee*) broccoli (*bro-co-li*)

brouette (*broo-eht*) wheelbarrow (*guil-ba-rrou*)

bureau (*bee-oo-roh*) desk (*desk*)

bus (*bee-oos*) bus (*baç*)

C

cabinet (*cah-bee-neh*) cabinet (*ca-bi-neth*)

cacahuète (*cah-cah-oo-eht*) peanut (*pi-nath*)

cachet (*cah-sheh*) stamp (*stemp*)

cactus (*cahc-toos*) cactus (*caktç*)

cadeau (*cah-doo*) gift (*ghifth*)

cadre (*cadr*) frame (*freim*)

cage (*cahgsh*) cage (*queich*)

caille (*cah-eel*) quail (*cuel*)

cambrioleur (*cohm-bree-oh-lehr*) burglar (*ber-gler*)

camion (*cah-mee-ohn*) truck (*track*)

canard (*cah-nahr*) duck (*dack*)

canari (*cah-nah-ree*) canary (*ke-ne-ri*)

canoë (*cah-noh-eh*) canoe (*ca-noo*)

cantaloup (*coh-tah-loo*) cantaloupe (*quen-ta-lop*)

carnet (*cahr-neh*) notebook (*nouth-book*)

carotte (*cahg-rroht*) carrot (*ke-rroth*)

carte (*cahrt*) map (*map*)

cascade (*cahs-cah-dah*) waterfall (*gua-der-fol*)

casque (*cahsk*) helmet (*'hel-meth*)

casse-noix (*cass/noh-ah*) nutcracker (*nath-krah-ker*)

céder (*ceh-deh*) yield (*iieldh*)

ceinture (*cehn-tee-oor*) belt (*belth*)

cerfs (*cehrg*) deer (*di-er*)

cerf-volant (*cehr/voo-loh*) kite (*ka-ith*)

cerise (*cehg-rees*) cherry (*che-rri*)

chacal (*shah-kahl*) jackal (*sha-kol*)

chaise (*chehz*) chair (*cher*)

chameau (*shah-moo*) camel (*ke-mol*)

champ (*shahmp*) field (*fi-old*)

champignon (*shahm-pee-nee-ohn*) mushroom (*mash-rrum*)

chandail (*sahn-dahl*) sweater (*sueh-rer*)

chandelle (*shan-dehll*) candle (*kehn-dol*)

chapeau (*shah-poo*) hat (*'hath*)

chariot (*shah-ree-oh*) wagon (*ua-gon*)

chat (*shah*) cat (*cath*)

château (*shah-too*) castle

chaton (*shah-toh*) kitten (*ki-rehn*)

chaussette (*shoh-oo-seht*) sock (*sock*)

chaussure (*shoh-see-oor*) shoe

chave-souris (*shah-veh/soo-ree*) bat (*bath*)

cheminée (*sheh-mee-neh*) chimney (*chim-ni*)

chemise (*cheh-miss*) shirt (*shert*)

chenil (*sheh-neel*) kennel (*ke-nol*)

chenille (*sheh-neel*) caterpillar (*ca-rer-pi-ler*)

cheval (*sheh-vahl*) horse (*'horç*)

chèvre (*shehvr*) goat (*go-uth*)

chien (*shee-eean*) dog (*dog*)

chimpanzé (*sheem-pahn-zee*) chimpanzee (*chim-pan-si*)

chiot (*she-oh*) puppy (*pa-pi*)

chocolat (*shoh-coh-lah*) chocolate (*cho-co-leh-ith*)

chou (*shoo*) cabbage (*ca-bech*)

cigogne (*see-goh-nee-eh*) stork (*stork*)

cirque (*seerk*) circus (*cir-cus*)

ciseaux (*see-soh*) scissors (*si-sorç*)

citron (*see-troh*) lemon (*le-mon*)

citrouille (*see-troh-ool*) pumpkin (*pahmp-kiihn*)

dauphin (*doh-phah*) dolphin (*dol-fin*)

dé (*deh*) dice (*da-iis*)

dent (*dohn*) tooth (*tuz*)

disque (*deesk*) disk (*disk*)

docteur (*dohc-tehr*) doctor (*doc-tor*)

échecs (*eh-shehk*) chess (*ché-s*)

échelle (*eh-shehl*) ladder (*lah-der*)

échelle (*eh-shehl*) scale (*s-kel*)

clé (*clee*) key (*kii*)

cloche (*clohsh*) bell (*bell*)

clôture (*cloh-tee-oor*) fence (*fénç*)

clown (*cloon*) clown (*clah-oun*)

coccinelle (*cohc-zee-nehl*) ladybug (*lei-di/bog*)

cochon (*coh-shohn*) pig (*pig*)

coeur (*kegr*) heart (*'harth*)

coing (*coo-ah*) quince (*cuh-iihnç*)

coléoptère (*coh-lee-ehp-tehrg*) beetle (*bi-rol*)

collier (*coh-lle-eh*) necklace (*neck-leis*)

concombre (*coh-coombr*) cucumber (*kiu-cum-ber*)

confiture (*coh-phee-tee-oor*) jam (*sham*)

coq (*cohk*) rooster (*russ-ter*)

coquille (*coh-kee-ah*) shell (*shell*)

corbeille (*cohr-beh-ee-eh*) basket (*baç-keth*)

corde (*cohgrd*) rope (*rohup*)

cordon (*cohrg-dohn*) ribbon (*ri-bon*)

D

doigt (*doo-ah*) finger (*fin-ger*)

domino (*doh-mee-noh*) domino (*do-mi-no*)

E

école (*eh-cohl*) school (*s-cul*)

écouteur (*eh-coo-tehr*) earphone (*ir-fon*)

écureuil (*eh-coo-roh-eel*) squirrel (*scuerl*)

église (*eh-gleez*) church (*cherch*)

élan (*eh-lohn*) elk (*elk*)

corne (*cohgrn*) horn (*'horn*)

cou (*coo*) neck (*neck*)

coude (*coh-ood*) elbow (*el-bou*)

couronne (*coh-rohn*) crown (*craun*)

couteau (*coo-toh*) knife (*knah-iif*)

cow-boy (*coh-oo/boo-ah*) cowboy (*cahu-bohi*)

crabe (*crahb*) crab (*crab*)

craquelin (*crahc-lah*) cracker (*cra-ker*)

cravate (*crah-vaht*) tie (*taii*)

crayon (*creh-ee-ohn*) pencil (*pehn-sol*)

crevette (*creh-veht*) shrimp (*shriimp*)

cric dans la boîte (*cree/dohn/lah/boo-aht*) jack in the box (*shack/in/deh/box*)

crocodile (*croh-coh-dree-leh*) crocodile (*cro-ca-drol*)

croix (*croo-ah*) cross (*croç*)

cruche (*croosh*) jog (*shog*)

cubes de glace (*coob/doo/glahs*) ice cubes (*aiiss-kiubss*)

cuillère (*coo-lee-ehr*) spoon (*spoon*)

douche (*doosh*) shower (*sha-goo-er*)

dragon (*drah-gohn*) dragon (*dra-gon*)

drapeau (*drah-poh*) flag (*flag*)

éléphant (*eh-leh-phahn*) elephant (*e-le-fanth*)

encens (*ohn-sah*) incense (*ii-ncéénss*)

envelopper (*ahn-veh-lo-peh*) envelop (*ehn-ve-lohp*)

épaule (*eh-poh-ool*) shoulder (*shohul-der*)

épée (*eh-peh*) sword (*suordh*)

épingle *(eh-pah-glah)* pin *(piihn)*

épingle de sûreté *(eh-pahn-gl/doh/see-oor-teh)* safety pin *(seif-ti/pin)*

faucon *(phoh-coh)* hawk *('hak)*; falcon *(fal-con)*

fée *(fee)* fairy *(fe-ri)*

fenêtre *(pheh-nehtr)* window *(u-iin-dou)*

fer *(fehr)* iron *(ah-ii-ron)*

fer à cheval *(fehr-ah-sheh-vahl)* horseshoe *('hors-shu)*

ferme *(fehrm)* farm *(farm)*

fermeture éclair *(fehr-meh-toohr/eh-clehr)* zipper *(zi-per)*

feu *(fehg)* fire *(fa-ior)*

feuille *(pheh-ee-eh)* leaf *(lif)*

gant *(gohn)* glove *(glouv)*

garage *(gah-rash)* garage *(gah-rash)*

gâteau *(gah-too)* cake *(keiik)*

gaufre *(gohfr)* waffle *(ua-fol)*

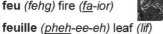

gazelle *(gah-zehl)* gazelle *(ga-zel)*

genoux *(sheh-noo)* knees *(kniiç)*

géranium *(sheh-rah-nee-oom)* geranium *(she-re-nium)*

hamac *(ah-mahk)* hammock *('ha-mek)*

hamburguer *(am-boor-gehr)* hamburger *('ham-bur-guer)*

hamster *(ahms-tehr)* hamster *(jams-ter)*

igloo *(ee-gloo)* igloo *(ah-ii-gloo)*

île *(eel)* island *(ah-ii-lahnd)*

escalator *(ehs-keh-lah-tohr)* escalator *(ehss-ca-leh-i-ror)*

escalier *(ehs-cah-lee-eh)* stair *(ster)*

F

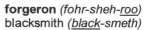

feuille d'érable *(pheh-eeoo/deh/rabl)* maple leaf *(mei-pol/lif)*

figue *(fee-geh)* fig *(fig)*

flamant *(flah-moh)* flamingo *(fla-min-go)*

flèche *(flehsh)* arrow *(e-rrou)*

fleur *(flehr)* flower *(fla-uer)*

foin *(phoo-ah)* hay *('he-ii)*

forêt *(foh-reh)* forest *(fo-resth)*

G

gilet *(she-leh)* vest *(vesth)*

girafe *(she-raph)* giraffe *(shi-raf)*

girouette météorologique *(she-oo-reht/meh-teh-oh-roh-loh-sheek)* weather vane *(que-der/veh-iihn)*

H

glace *(glahss)* ice cream *(ah-*

haricots de gelée *(ah-ree-coh/deh/sheh-leh)* jelly beans *(she-li/bihnss)*jelly fish *(she-li/fish)*

harpe *(ahrp)* harp *('harp)*

herbe *(ehrb)* grass *(grass)*

hérisson *(eh-ree-sohn)* hedge-hog *('hedsh-'hog)*

I

ingénieur *(ahn-she-nee-ehr)* engineer *(en-shi-nier)*

escargot *(ehs-cahr-goh)* snail *(sneil)*

esquimau *(ehs-kee-moh)* eskimo *(ehss-ki-mo)*

forgeron *(fohr-sheh-roo)* blacksmith *(black-smeth)*

fougère *(foo-shehr)* fern *(fern)*

fourchette *(foor-sheht)* fork *(fork)*

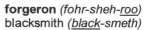

fourmi *(phor-mee)* ant *(ahnth)*

fraise *(phreh-sah)* strawberry *(s-tro-be-rri)*

framboise *(frahm-boo-ehs)* raspberry *(rasp-be-rri)*

fromage *(froh-magsh)* cheese *(chiiss)*

fruit *(phroo-ee)* fruit *(fruth)*

gladioulus *(glah-dee-oh-lee)* gladioulus *(gla-dio-los)*

globe *(glohb)* globe *(glob)*

grange *(grahnsh)* barn *(barn)*

grenouille *(grah-noo-lleh)* frog *(frog)*

guépard *(geh-pahgr)* cheetah *(chi-ra)*

guêpe *(gehp)* wasp *(guasp)*

guitare *(gee-tahr)* guitar *(gui-tar)*

guitare hawaïenne *(gee-tahr/ah-ee-ehn)* ukulele *(io-ko-leh-leh)*

hibou *(ee-boo)* owl *(ah-ul)*

homard *(oh-mahs)* lobster *(lobç-ter)*

horloge *(ohr-lohsh)* clock *(clock)*

houe *(oh-oo)* hoe *('ho-oo)*

iris *(ee-rees)* iris *(ah-ii-riiç)*

73

jaguar *(shah-<u>glah</u>)* jaguar *(<u>sha</u>-gooar)*

jambe *(shamb)* leg *(leg)*

jambon *(<u>shahm</u>-boh)* ham *('ham)*

jaquette *(shah-keht)* jacket *(<u>sha</u>-keth)*

jardin *(shahr-<u>dehn</u>)* garden *(<u>gar</u>-dehn)*

jarre *(shagr)* jar *(<u>shar</u>)*

jazmin *(<u>shahs</u>-mah)* jazmin *(<u>shaç</u>-min)*

jean *(shoh)* jeans *(shihnç)*

jockey *(<u>shoh</u>-keh)* jockey *(<u>sho</u>-ki)*

journal *(<u>shohr</u>-nahl)* newspaper *(<u>niuss</u>-pei-per)*

jungle *(shahngl)* jungle *(<u>shan</u>-gol)*

jupe *(shoop)* skirt *(skerth)*

jus *(shoo)* juice *(shuç)*

kangourou *(kahn-goh-<u>roo</u>)* kangaroo *(<u>kehn</u>-ghe-roo)*

karaté *(kah-rah-<u>teh</u>)* karate *(ka-<u>ra</u>-ri)*

kayac *(<u>keh</u>-yahc)* kayak *(<u>kah</u>-iak)*

ketchup *(<u>keht</u>-choop)* ketchup *(<u>keth</u>-chop)*

labyrinthe *(lah-bee-<u>rahnt</u>)* labyrinth *(la-ba-<u>riiith</u>)*

lacet *(lah-<u>ceh</u>)* lace *(leiiç)*

laine *(lehn)* wool *(wul)*

lait *(leh)* milk *(milk)*

laitue *(<u>leh</u>-too)* lettuce *(<u>le</u>-rooç)*

lampe *(lohm)* lamp *(lahmp)*

lampe de poche *(lahmp/deh/pohsh)* flashlight *(flash-lahith)*

lapin *(<u>lah</u>-pah)* rabbit *(<u>ra</u>-bith)*

laurier *(<u>loh</u>-ree-eh)* laurel *(<u>lohu</u>-rol)*

lavande *(<u>lah</u>-voh)* lavender *(<u>leh</u>-ii-vahn-der)*

léopard *(<u>leh</u>-oh-pahr)* leopard *(<u>le</u>-perd)*

lèvres *(lehvr)* lips *(<u>li</u>-ps)*

lézard *(<u>leh</u>-zahr)* lizard *(<u>li</u>zahrd)*

lièvre *(lee-<u>ehvr</u>)* hare *('her)*

lilas *(<u>lee</u>-lah)* lilac *(<u>lah</u>-ii-lac)*

lion *(lee-<u>oh</u>)* lion *(<u>la</u>-ion)*

lion marin *(lee-<u>ohn</u>/<u>mah</u>-rah)* sea lion *(si/<u>la</u>-ion)*

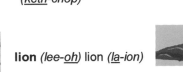

lit *(lee)* bed *(bedh)*

livre *(leevr)* book *(book)*

loup *(loo)* wolf *(wuf)*

luge *(loogsh)* sled *(sledh)*

lune *(lloonn)* moon *(mun)*

lunettes de soleil *(loo-<u>neht</u>/deh/soh/<u>lee</u>-ehl)* sunglasses *(<u>san</u>-gla-ses)*

lynx *(lahnxz)* lynx *(<u>lihnkzss</u>)*

magazine *(mah-gah-<u>zeen</u>)* magazine *(<u>ma</u>-ga-zíne)*

magicien *(<u>mah</u>-she-see-ah)* magician *(ma-<u>gi</u>-shian)*

magnolia *(mah-nee-<u>oh</u>-lee-ah)* magnolia *(mag-<u>no</u>-lia)*

main *(mah)* hand *('hahnd)*

maïs *(<u>meh</u>-eez)* corn *(corn)*

maison *(meh-<u>sohn</u>)* house *('haus)*

mammouth *(mah-<u>moot</u>)* mammoth *(<u>me</u>-moç)*

mandarine *(mohn-dah-<u>reen</u>)* mandarin *(<u>mehn</u>-da-ríhn)*

mangue *(mohng)* mango *(<u>meh</u>-iihn-go)*

marguerite *(mahr-geh-<u>reet</u>)* daisy *(<u>dei</u>-si)*

marteau *(mahr-<u>too</u>)* hammer *('ha-mer)*

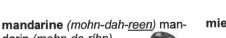

masque *(mahsk)* mask *(mask)*

médaille *(<u>meh</u>-dah-il)* medal *(<u>me</u>-dal)*

melon *(<u>meh</u>-loh)* melon *(<u>me</u>-lohn)*

météore *(<u>mee</u>-teh-ohr)* meteor *(<u>mi</u>-ri-or)*

meubles *(<u>meh</u>-oo-bleh)* furniture *(<u>for</u>-ni-chur)*

miel *(mee-<u>ehl</u>)* honey *('<u>ha</u>-ni)*

miroir *(mee-rroo-<u>ah</u>)* mirror *(<u>mi</u>-rror)*

moineau *(moo-<u>eh</u>-noo)* sparrow *(spe-rrou)*

molaire *(moh-<u>lehr</u>)* molaire molar *(<u>mohu</u>-ler)*

moniteur *(moh-nee-<u>tehr</u>)* monitor *(<u>mo</u>-ni-rer)*

montagne *(mohn-<u>tahg</u>-nee-ah)* mountain *(<u>moun</u>-ten)*

montée *(<u>mohn</u>-teh)* uphill *(ap-hil)*

montre *(mohntr)* watch *(guatch)*

mouche *(<u>moh</u>-oosh)* fly *(flahi)*

mouchoir (_moo_-shoo-ah) handkerchief ('_hahnd_-ker-kif)

mouette (moo-_eht_) gull (_goh_-ul)

mouette (moo-_eht_) seagull (_si_-gul)

navire (_nah_-vee-ahr) ship (shiip)

neige (nehsh) snow (snou)

nez (neh) nose (nohuç)

nid (nee) nest (nesth)

oeil (_oh_-eel) eye (ah-ih)

oeillet (oh-lee-eh) carnation (_car_-nei-shion)

oeuf (_oh_-ooph) egg (egg)

oie (oo-_ah_) goose (guç)

oignon (_ohg_-nee-ohn) onion (_o_-ni-ohn)

oiseau (oo-_eh_-soo) bird (berdh)

ombrelle (ohm-_brehl_) parasol (_per_-a-sol)

pain (pah) bread (bredh)

panda (_pohn_-dah) panda (_pan_-da)

panthère (_pahn_-tehgr) panther (_pan_-ter)

papillon (pah-pee-yon) butterfly (_ba_-rer-flai)

parachute (pah-rah-_shoot_) parachute (_per_-a-_shuth_)

parapluie (pah-rah-_plee_) umbrella (am-_bréh_-la)

passeport (_pahss_-pohr) passport (_pass_-port)

passoire (pah-ee-soo-_ah_) strainer (_stri_-ner)

pastèque (pahs-_tehk_) watermelon (_gua_-der-meh-lohn)

patate (pah-_taht_) yam (iiam)

patins (_pah_-tehn) ice skates (_ais_-skeitç)

paume (pahgm) palm (palm)

N

Noël (noh-_ehl_) X-mas (_criiss_-maç)

noix (noh-_ah_) nut (nath)

O

ongle (oongl) nail (neil)

orange (_ohg_-rahnsh) orange (_o_-ransh)

orchidée (ohr-_kee_-dee) orchid (_or_-quid)

P

pêche (pehsh) peach (pich)

peigne (peh-ee-neh) comb (kohmb)

peinture (peh-een-_toor_) paint (_peh_-iinth)

pélican (_peh_-lee-cohn) pelican (_pe_-li-cahn)

pelle (pehll) shovel (_sha_-vol)

pensée (pohn-_seh_) pansy (_pen_-si)

perroquet (peh-rroh-_keh_) parrot (_pe_-rroth)

perruche (pehg-rroosh) parakeet (_per_-kith)

perruches inséparables (peh-roo-shehg/ehn-see-pah-_rah_-ble) lovebirds (_lov_-berdss)

perruque (peh-_rook_) wig (uiig)

persil (_pehr_-see) parsley (_pars_-li)

phare (phah) lighthouse (_la_-ith-'ha-hus)

---

moustaches (_moos_-tahsh) whiskers (_uiss_-kerss)

moutons (moo-_tohn_) sheep (shiip)

mûre (meegr) blackberry (_blak_-be-rri)

noix de coco (noo-_eh_/deh/_coh_-coh) coconut (_co_-co-not)

noix de pecan (noo-_ah_/dee/_pee_-cahn) pecan (pi-can)

nuage (nahsh) cloud (_clah_-oud)

oreille (oh-_reh_-eel) ear (_i_-ahr)

oreiller (oh-_rrehg_-ee-eh) pillow (_pi_-lou)

ornement (_ohr_-neh-moh) bulb (bolb)

os (ohs) bone (boh-un)

ours (ohrs) bear (ber)

ours de koala (oors/deh/koo-_eh_-lah) koala bear (koh-_ah_-lah/ber)

ours polaire (oors/poo-_lehr_) polar bear (po-lar/beerr)

piano (pee-_ah_-noh) piano (_pia_-no)

pichet (pee-sheh) pitcher (_pit_-cher)

pickles (_pee_-kehls) pickle (_pi_-col)

pieds (pee-_eh_) feet (fiith)

pieuvre (pee-_ehvr_) octopus (_oc_-tuh-puhss)

pigeon (_pee_-shohn) pigeon (_pi_-shih-on)

pin (pah) pine (pain)

pingouin (_pehn_-goo-ah) penguin (_pen_-guin)

planche de surf (plahnsh/deh/sehrf) surf-board (_sorf_-bord)

plateau *(plah-toh)* tray *(trei)*

platypus *(plah-tee-poo)* platypus *(pla-ri-puss)*

plume *(plee-oom)* feather *(féh-der)*

poêle *(poh-ehl)* skillet *(ski-leth)*

poignet *(pohg-nee-eh)* wrist *(rist)*

poing *(poo-ahng)* fist *(fist)*

poire *(poo-ahr)* pear *(peerr)*

poisson *(poo-eh-sohn)* fish *(fish)*

poisson de gelée *(poo-ah-sohn/deh-sheh-leh)* jelly fish *(she-li-fish)*

raccon *(rah-coo)* raccoon *(ra-coohn)*

racine *(rah-seenn)* root *(ruth)*

radio *(rah-dee-oh)* radio *(rei-dio)*

radis *(rah-dee)* radish *(ra-dish)*

raisins *(reh-sahn)* grapes *(greipç)*

rame *(rahm)* oar *(oiiar)*

raquette *(rah-keht)* racket *(ra-queth)*

rasoir *(reh-soo-ah)* razor *(reii-zor)*

rat *(rah)* rat *(rath)*

ratisser *(rah-tee-seh)* rake *(reiik)*

sablier *(sah-blee-ehr)* hourglass *(aur-glaç)*

sac *(sahk)* bag *(bag)*

sac à dos *(sahc-eh-doh)* backpack *(back-pack)*

sac à main *(sahk/ah/mah)* handbag *('hand-bahg)*

salamandre *(sah-lah-mahndr)* salamander *(sal-a-mehn-der)*

sandale *(sohn-dahl)* sandal *(sahn-dal)*

saucisse *(soh-sees)* sausage *(so-sech)*

76

---

pomme *(pohm)* apple *(a-pol)*

pomme de pin *(pohm/deh/pah)* pinecone *(pah-iihn-cohn)*

pomme de terre *(pohm/deh/tehrr)* potato *(po-teii-ro)*

poney *(poo-neh)* pony *(po-ni)*

porte *(pohrt)* door *(door)*

porte *(pohrt)* gate *(ghehith)*

portefeuille *(pohr-teh-pheh-eel)* wallet *(wa-let)*

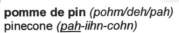

quart de dollar *(cahrt/deh/doh-llahr)* quarter *(cuh-oh-ra)*

Rayons X *(rah-ee-ohn/dees)* X-ray *(ex-reii)*

réfrigérateur *(reh-phree-sheh-rah-tohr)* refrigerator *(re-fri-shi-reii-rohr)*

règle *(reh-gl)* ruler *(ru-ler)*

reine *(reh-een)* queen *(quh-iihn)*

remuez le puzzle d'affaissement *(reh-mee-ooeh/leh/pozz/dah-fees-mah)* jig sag puzzle *(zig/saoo/(zig/saoo/pá-zol)*

sauterelle *(soo-trehl)* grasshopper *(gras-ho-per)*

savon *(sah-vohn)* soap *(sohup)*

scooter *(scoo-tehr)* scooter *(scu-rer)*

scorpion *(scohr-pee-ohn)* scorpion *(scor-pion)*

seau *(soo)* bucket *(ba-keth)*

serpent *(sehr-pohn)* snake *(sneik)*

serrure *(seh-rroor)* lock *(lock)*

serviette *(sehr-vee-eht)* towel *(ta-uel)*

---

pot *(poh)* pot *(poth)*

pouce *(poos)* thumb *(zahm)*

poule *(pooll)* hen *('hehn)*

poulet *(poo-leh)* chicken *(chi-kehn)*

poupée *(poo-peh)* doll *(dohll)*

présent *(preh-sohn)* present *(pre-senth)*

prise d'eau *(prees-d'oo)* hydrant *('ha-ii-drahnth)*

prison *(pree-sohn)* jail *(sheil)*

prix *(pree)* award *(a-oird)*

prune *(proonn)* plum *(plam)*

renard *(reh-nahr)* fox *(fox)*

renne *(rehn)* reindeer *(reiihn-diiehr)*

rhinocéros *(ree-noh-ceh-rohs)* rhinoceros *(rai-no-ceh-rehç)*

robe *(rohb)* dress *(dress)*

robinet *(roh-bee-neh)* faucet *(fo-cet)*

robot *(roh-boh)* robot *(ruh-both)*

roche *(rohsh)* rock *(rock)*

rose *(rohgs)* rose *(roh-us)*

rossignol *(roh-see-nee-ohl)* nightingale *(nahii-tiihn-ghel)*

roue *(roo)* wheel *(ui-ol)*

serviettes *(sehr-vee-ehts)* napkins *(nap-kinss)*

short *(shohrt)* shorts *(shortss)*

sifflet *(see-pleh)* whistle *(ui-sol)*

singe *(sahnsh)* monkey *(mon-ki)*

sofa *(soh-phah)* sofa *(sohu-fa)*

soleil *(soh-leh-eel)* sun *(sahn)*

souci *(soh-see)* marigold *(me-ri-gold)*

souris *(soo-ree)* mouse *(mahooss)*

stylo *(stee-loh)* pen *(pehn)*

sucette *(she -oo-ceht)* lollipop *(lo-li-pop)*

T

table (_tah_-blah) table (_tei_-bol)

tambour (_tahm_-boor) drum (drom)

tapis (_tah_-pee) carpet (_car_-pet)

tasse (tahss) cup (cap)

taupe (tohp) mole (moul)

téléphone (teh-leh-_phohn_) - telephone (_te_-le-fon)

télescope (_teh_-lehs-cohp) telescope (_te_-les-cop)

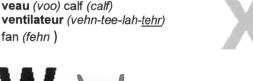

télévision (teh-leh-vee-shee-_ohn_) television (te-le-_vi_-shion)

tente (tohnt) tent (tenth)

terre (tehrr) earth (erth)

terrine (teh-_ree_-nah) bowl (boh-ool)

tête (teht) head ('hed)

théière (teh-ee-_ehr_) teapot (_tii_-poth)

tigre (tee-gr) tiger (_tai_-ger)

tilleul (_tee_-lee-ohl) lime (_lah_-iim)

tomate (toh-_maht_) tomato (to-_mehii_-ro)

tondeuse à gazon (toon-dehs/ah/gah-zohn) **lawn mower** (lan-_moh_-er)

toasteur (_toos_-tehr) toaster (_tous_-ter)

toile d'araignée (too-ehl/dahg-_rahg_-nee-eh) cobweb (_cob_-web)

U

ver (vehr) worm (uorm)

verre à pied (vehrr/ah/pee-_ehd_) goblet (_ga_-bleth)

verres (vehrr) glasses (_gla_-seç)

viande (vee-ahnd) meat (mith)

vigne (_veeg_-nee-eh) vine (va-iinn)

X

xylophone (see-loh-_phohn_)

W

walkie-film-parlant (vahl-kee/pheelm/pahr-_lohn_) walkie-talkie (_ua_-kii/_tol_-kii)

zèbre (zehbr) zebra (_zi_-bra)

Z

zebu (_zeh_-booh) zebu (_zi_-bu)

toile d'araignée (too-_ehl_/dah-rag-nee-_eh_) spiderweb (_speii_-der-web)

toit (too-_ah_) roof (ruf)

torche (torsh) torch (torch)

tortue (_tohr_-too) turtle (_to_-rrol)

toucan (_too_-cohn) toucan (_tu_-ken)

tour (toor) tower (_tah_-uehr)

tournesol (toor-neh-_sohl_) sunflower (_sahn_-fla-uerr)

tournevis (_tohr_-neh-vees) screwdriver (_scru_-drah-ii-ver)

tourte (too-_ohrt_) pie (pahi)

train (trahn) train (_tré_-iin)

trompette (_troo_-peht) trumpet (_trom_-peth)

u-tour (ee-_oo_/toor) u-turn (_iu_-torn)

viole (vee-_ohl_) violet (_va_-io-leth)

violon (vee-oh-_lohn_) violin (va-io-liihn)

visage (vee-_sash_) face (_feh_-ihç)

visière (vee-see-_ehr_) visor (_vahii_-sor)

volcan (vohl-_cahn_) volcano (vol-_keii_-no)

volet (voh-_leh_) shutter (_sha_-rer)

Y

yacht (ee-_oht_) yacht (iiahth)

yogourt (ee-_oh_-goor) yogurt (io-gurth)

zigzag (zeeg-_zahg_) zigzag (zig-zag)

V

vache (vahsh) cow (kahu)

vague (vahg) wave (uehiiv)

valve (vahlv) valve (valve)

vase (vahs) vase (veiiç)

veau (voo) calf (calf)

ventilateur (vehn-tee-lah-_tehr_) fan (fehn)

THE ALPHABET
(di/al-fa-beth)

L'ALPHABET
(lehl/phah-beht)

(ehii) A *(ah)*	*(ehn)* N *(ehn)*
(bii) B *(beh)*	*(o-u)* O *(oh)*
(si) C *(ceh)*	*(pi)* P *(peh)*
(di) D *(deh)*	*(kiu)* Q *(coo)*
(i) E *(eo)*	*(ahr)* R *(ehr)*
(ef) F *(ehf)*	*(ehss)* S *(ehss)*
(gi) G *(sheh)*	*(ti)* T *(teh)*
(eiich) H *(ahsh)*	*(iu)* U *(ee)*
(ahii) I *(ee)*	*(vi)* V *(veh)*
(gehii) J *(she)*	*(da-bliu)* W *(dob-bleh/veh)*
(kehii) K *(kah)*	*(ex)* X *(eexs)*
(el) L *(ehl)*	*(guahii)* Y *(ee/gah-eek)*
(ehm) M *(ehm)*	*(zi)* Z *(zehd)*

THE NUMBERS
(di/nam-berss)

LES NOMBRES
(leh/nohmbr)

one *(guhán)*	1	un *(ahn)*
two *(chu)*	2	deux *(doo)*
three *(tri)*	3	trois *(troo-ah)*
four *(for)*	4	quatre *(catr)*
five *(fahiiv)*	5	cinq *(senk)*
six *(siixss)*	6	six *(sees)*
seven *(seh-vehn)*	7	sept *(seht)*
eight *(eiith)*	8	huit *(oo-eet)*
nine *(na-iihn)*	9	neuf *(nehf)*
ten *(tehn)*	10	dix *(dees)*

THE COLORS
(di/co-lorss)

LES COULEURS
(leh/coo-lehr)

red *(red)*	rouge *(roosh)*
orange *(o-ransh)*	orange *(ohg-rahnsh)*
yellow *(ieh-lou)*	jaune *(shoon)*
green *(griihn)*	vert *(vehr)*
blue *(bleu)*	bleu *(bloo)*
purple *(por-pol)*	pourpre *(poorp)*
pink *(piihnk)*	rose *(rohgs)*
grey *(grehii)*	gris *(gree)*
black *(black)*	noir *(noo-ah)*
white *(uahiith)*	blanc *(bloh)*

THE FAMILY
(di/fa-mi-li)

LA FAMILLE
(lah/fah-mee-ee-ah)

father *(fa-der)*	père *(pehr)*
mother *(ma-der)*	mère *(mehr)*
son *(san)*	fils *(phees)*
daughter *(do-ra)*	fille *(phee-ah)*
brother *(bra-der)*	frère *(phrehr)*
sister *(sis-tehr)*	soeur *(sehr)*
grandfather *(grand-fa-der)*	grand-père *(grahnd-pehr)*
grandmother *(grand-ma-der)*	grand-mère *(grahnd-mehr)*
grandson *(grand-son)*	petit-fils *(peh-tee/fees)*
granddaughter *(grand-do-ra)*	petite-fille *(peh-teet/phee-ah)*

78

THE DAYS OF THE WEEK
(di/deis/of-di-wik)

LES JOURS DE LA SEMAINE
(leh/shoors/dee/lah/seh-mahnn)

Monday *(man-dei)*
Tuesday *(tiuss-dahi)*
Wednesday *(uehnss-dai)*
Thursday *(terss-dai)*
Friday *(frahi-dehi)*
Saturday *(sa-rur-dahii)*
Sunday *(san-dei)*

Lundi *(lahn-dee)*
Mardi *(mahr-dee)*
Mercredi *(mehr-creh-dee)*
Jeudi *(shoo-dee)*
Vendredi *(vahn-dreh-dee)*
Samedi *(sah-mee-dee)*
Dimanche *(dee-mahnsh)*

THE MONTHS OF THE YEAR
(di/mohnthss/ohf/deh/ii-ar)

LES MOIS DE L'ANNÉE
(leh/moo-ah/deel/ah-neh)

January *(sha-niu-e-ri)*
February *(fe-bru-ei-ri)*
March *(march)*
April *(eii-prohl)*
May *(meii)*
June *(shoon)*
July *(shu-lahii)*
August *(au-gost)*
September *(sehp-tem-ber)*
October *(oc-toh-ber)*
November *(no-vem-ber)*
December *(di-sem-ber)*

Janvier *(shan-vee-eh)*
Février *(feh-vreh-ee-eh)*
Mars *(mahrs)*
Avril *(ah-vreel)*
Mai *(meh)*
Juin *(shoo-ah)*
Juillet *(shoo-llee-eh)*
Août *(oot)*
Septembre *(sehp-tahmbr)*
Octobre *(ohc-toh-bah)*
Novembre *(noh-vohmbr)*
Décembre *(dee-cehmbr)*

THE SEASONS
(di/si-sonss)

LES SAISONS
(leh/see/sohn)

Spring *(es-pring)*

Fall *(fol)*

Summer *(sa-mer)*

Winter *(uiihn-ter)*

Printemps *(prehn-tahm)*

Automne *(oo-tohn)*

Été *(eh-teh)*

Hiver *(ee-vehr)*

LaVergne, TN USA
05 March 2010
175115LV00004B